Draw & Writ

The idea of this journal is to have fun and let creativity flow. But before we start, here are five top tips to get the most out this book.

1. Body basics

Good posture is important for writing. Encourage children to sit with their feet flat on the floor, their back straight (no heads on the table) and relaxed shoulders.

2. Think Ink

Although children usually write in pencil at school, it can be useful for them to start handwriting with felt tips and gel pens, which have a nice, fluid delivery of ink.

3. B prepared

If your child is using a pencil, the softer B pencils are generally easier to write with as they move more fluently across the page.

4. Get a grip

Keep an eye on the child's pencil grip. It's important that the pad of the thumb connects with the pencil. If the side or tip of the thumb touches, it closes up the hand and restricts the flow of movement.

5. Let's twist

The child may find writing easier if their paper is at an angle. You can turn the page up to 45 degrees in either direction.

Now let's get creative!

Made in the USA
Columbia, SC
13 September 2020

20690719R00061